PIES and TARTS
with Schmecks Appeal

EDNA STAEBLER

McGraw-Hill Ryerson
Montreal   Toronto

McClelland & Stewart
Toronto

First published in 1990 by

McGRAW-HILL RYERSON LIMITED
330 Progress Avenue
Toronto, Canada
M1P 2Z5

McCLELLAND & STEWART LIMITED
481 University Avenue
Toronto, Canada
M5G 2E9

ISBN: 077108283-5

1 2 3 4 5 6 7 8 9 0   W   9 8 7 6 5 4 3 2 1 0

Printed and bound in Canada

 This book was manufactured using acid-free paper.

Canadian Cataloguing in Publication Data

Staebler, Edna,   – date
   Pies and tarts with schmecks appeal

(Schmecks appeal cookbook series)
ISBN 0-7710-8283-5

1. Pastry.   2. Cookery, Mennonite.   3. Cookery –
Ontario – Waterloo (Regional municipality).
I. Title.   II. Series: Staebler, Edna,   – date

Schmecks appeal cookbook series.

TX773.S73 1990   641.8′ 652   C90-094258-4

CONTENTS

PIES

Sometimes pies appear on Bevvy Martin's table three times a day. Every Friday she and her daughter Salome bake twenty pies and store them in the cellar. Because as many as thirty-five vistors may come to their house after church on Sunday, the pies may all be used at once; if not, there'll be enough pies to last throughout the week. Their variety is infinite: besides all the fruit, custard, and mince pies, there are sour cream, raisin, tomato, schnitz, apple butter, cottage cheese, buttermilk, and funeral pies, and others made up on the spur of the moment to keep things from being wasted. It is not surprising that the Pennsylvania Dutch are credited with inventing the double-crust pie.

In the winter, without fail, Bevvy makes shoofly, botzelbaum (somersault), and gravel pies. She calls them cake-pies because they have a touch of soda in them, and their crumbly-topped fillings stay moist yet do not soak into the crust. They are put on the table at breakfast and taste especially good dunked in coffee.

When I asked Amsey which pie is his favourite, he said, "Peach pie made with the peelings."

Bevvy smiled shyly. "We make it sometimes with the peelings after we do the canning. You know how sometimes the peaches don't peel too well and a little bit of the flesh sticks yet? Well, we just boil it with sugar and a little water till it's almost like jam, then we put it in a baked pie shell and cover it with whipped cream or boiled custard."

Amsey rolled his big brown eyes. "And that really schmecks."

May I immodestly add: my sisters and nieces make wonderful pies, too — and some of my own aren't bad, either. In a lifetime of living in Waterloo County I've encountered so many fantastic pies that they deserve a book of their own.

I think every pie is a winner. Some are Old Order Mennonite specials that you won't find in any other cookbook. A few are for company only — too rich or fancy

1

for everyday fare. The rest are just great schmecksy favourites of my family and friends.

Can you resist Eva's Backwood Pie, Lemon Apple, Pear Streusel, Five-Star Peach, Peanut Molasses (from Guyana), Glazed Fresh Strawberry Tarte, Kentucky Derby Pie, Southern Pecan (from a New Orleans friend), Crème de Menthe, Satan's Choice, and Raspberry Angel?

Pie Crusts

I never could make a good pie crust. My crusts were always tough or crumbly, no matter what recipe I'd try. Whenever we had a family get-together and I'd offer to make a pie, my sister or my niece would say, "No, Ednie, don't bother. You bring the vegetables. I'll make a pie."

But since my sister Norm gave me her recipe for a pat-in pie crust, I've had incredible success! Every time! The family no longer rejects my offerings. My crusts are crisp and tasty and golden. The edges may not be perfectly fluted as Norm's are but that's not important. Pat-in crust is so easy to make. I put all the ingredients into my food processor, give them a brief whirl, and pour the mixture into a pie plate. I pat it in firmly — around the edges first, then through the middle — and that's it. No rolling or wasting bits of pastry, and so fast it can be done in five minutes.

Norm doesn't mix her crust in her food processor. She lets her husband, Ralph, blend the ingredients with a fork in the pie plate. Then he can proudly say he made it. . . .

SPEEDY PAT-IN PASTRY

This is the pat-in pastry recipe that has revolutionized my pie-baking life. Since it was given to Norm by her friend Norma, she hasn't made pastry any other way. Nor have I. It's crisp, tender, tasty, and needs no finicky rolling.

1½ cups flour
1½ teaspoons sugar
¾ teaspoon salt
½ cup oil
3 tablespoons cold milk

Sift the flour, sugar, and salt directly into a 9-inch pie plate or into your food processor. Combine the oil and milk; beat with a fork until creamy. Pour all at once over the flour; give your food processor a brief whirl — or in the pie plate mix with a fork until the flour is completely dampened. Pat the dough with your fingers to line the sides and bottom of the pie plate. Flute the edges, then fill with whatever filling you've chosen. If you are making a baked shell to be filled later, prick the entire surface of the pastry with a fork to keep it from bubbling. Bake at 425°F for 15 minutes or until golden.

EXTENDING A PIE

When my lively cousin Ada called on me the other day, she said, "My niece is getting married and I want to give her a copy of your cookbook *More Food That Really Schmecks* because it has the recipe for pat-in pastry. I use it all the time — never bother now with any other. If I want a pie to serve more than six or eight, I pat the pastry into a 9" x 13" cake pan, spread the filling over it, and when it is baked, I cut it into 12 squares."

Because pie plates vary in size, you may have to adjust the recipe. Most recipes are for 9-inch pies. Mother had old-fashioned, shallow, 10-inch graniteware pans. When Norm bakes a pie for our extended family, she uses a rather deep 10-inch pan, and Ralph serves 8 to 10 pieces from it.

BASIC PIE CRUST

There are many ways to make pie crust: stick to your own method if you have one you like or try this fairly rich, tender, easy way.

For a 9-inch double crust pie (or six tart shells)

2 cups flour
1 teaspoon salt
⅔ cup shortening
¼ cup cold water — or less

Sift flour with salt into a bowl. Cut in shortening with 2 knives, a pastry blender, or your electric mixer until particles are the size of small peas. (If you like, you can double the recipe and store part in a covered jar in your fridge.) When ready to use, sprinkle the flour-shortening mixture with ice-cold water and mix lightly with a fork. Use only enough water to make a pastry ball that can be cleaned easily from the bowl. Roll on a lightly floured canvas or board.

The best church-social pie baker of Wilmot Township tells me that instead of water in her pie crust she uses sour cream with a ½ teaspoon of soda dissolved in it.

BARBIE'S PERFECT PASTRY

Barbie bakes lots of pies. This recipe makes 4 shells. Barbie keeps 3 or 4 of them in her freezer and fills one in a jiffy when she wants a pie for dinner.

2 cups lard
6 cups flour, half pastry, half all-purpose
2 teaspoons salt
1 teaspoon baking power
1 egg
1 tablespoon vinegar
Water to fill up the cup

Blend the lard, flour, salt, and baking powder with a pastry blender until the mix is fairly fine. In a measuring cup beat 1 egg and 1 tablespoon of vinegar; add enough water to fill up the cup. Add this to the flour mixture, mix gently with a fork. Don't work with it any more than you have to.

Bake filled pies at 450°F for 15 minutes then reduce to 350°F.

GRAHAM WAFER CRUST

Wonderful under a cream pie.

16 graham wafers (1½ cups)
½ cup sugar
½ cup softened butter
1 teaspoon flour
1 teaspoon cinnamon (optional)

Finely crush the wafers then combine them with the remaining ingredients and blend thoroughly. Press a bit more than half the mixture firmly to the bottom and sides of a well-buttered pie plate. Sprinkle the remaining crumbs over the meringue that covers your cream pie. Bake in a slow oven — 300°F — until lightly browned for about 20 minutes.

BUTTER-PECAN CRUST

Marg Curry served this at a ladies' luncheon. The filling was fresh glazed strawberries slathered with whipped cream. But you could use this crust whenever you want to be impressive.

½ cup butter
1 cup flour
¼ cup sugar
⅓ cup chopped pecans

Blend together butter, flour, and sugar until the mixture is crumbly. Stir in pecans. Press the mixture into a 9-inch pie plate and bake at 375°F for 12 to 15 minutes. Extravagant but delicious.

Try this with other nuts — almonds, brazils, walnuts — chopped with a knife.

COOKIE CRUMB CRUST FOR UNBAKED PIE

Try this with graham wafers, gingersnaps, vanilla wafers, or chocolate wafers — very finely crumbled. It's quick, easy, and has more flavour than pastry.

> **1½ cups cookie crumbs**
> **⅓ or ½ cup sugar**
> **⅓ to ½ cup melted butter**

Combine the crumbs with the sugar and melted butter. Press the mixture firmly against the bottom and sides of the pie plate, using the back of a spoon. Bake for 10 to 15 minutes at 300°F.

MERINGUE PIE SHELL

When Norm entertains, she loves to make glamorous desserts that would make her guests obese if they weren't a one-time treat. Her favourite is a meringue crust into which she pours various irresistible fillings: chocolate or rum with almonds, ice cream with fresh peaches or strawberries, lemon filling, or pineapple and nuts in whipped cream. Her meringue is light, crisp, and never embarrassing to chew or cut with a fork.

> **⅔ cup egg whites at room temperature**
> **(about 4 large eggs)**
> **1 cup white sugar**
> **1¼ teaspoons vinegar**
> **1¼ teaspoons water**
> **½ teaspoon almond flavouring**
> **⅛ teaspoon salt**

Beat all the ingredients together till they are really stiff and glossy — better overdo it than underbeat it. Spread evenly in a well-buttered pan. Preheat the oven to 400°F and *turn it off*. Put the pie into the oven and forget about it till the oven is cold — overnight is a good time. The shell will be pale beige. If it has cracked, the oven was too hot; if it is tough, it was too cool. But that never happens to Norm's. All she has to do on the day of the party is put the filling into the shell. The meringue will keep for days in a dry place.

Toppings For Pies

*One day my friends Eva and Hannah and I sat at
Hannah's kitchen table and talked about pies while we
drank tea, ate jam-jams, and a piece of pear streusel pie
that Hannah had made in the morning.*

*I wrote down the recipes for their favourite Mennonite
pies as they read them from their hand-written notebooks,
which have only lists of ingredients. Eva and Hannah have
made so many pies that they need no directions. "You just
make the dough, put in the filling, sprinkle it with crumbs
and bake it till it's done," they told me.*

"What about a top crust or a lattice?" I asked them.

*"For some pies we do that, but crumbs have more taste
and are easier to make," Hannah said. "Sometimes I mix
up a big batch and keep it in the fridge."*

*"For lemon or chocolate or pies like that, I have a
meringue recipe that stays perfect," Eva said.*

*Hannah grinned. "And just before we serve a fruit pie we
usually cover it with whipped cream. That's the best."*

CRUMB OR STREUSEL TOPPING

If you use pat-in pastry (page 3) to make a pie, you won't have a top crust. A crumb topping is a great substitute. Golden and crumbly, it looks irresistible, has a warm, buttery flavour, and is easy to make. It can be used with any fruit pie and some others as well.

> ½ cup brown sugar
> ¼ to ½ cup flour
> ¼ to ½ cup butter or margarine
>   (but butter is better)
> ¼ cup chopped nuts, coconut, or rolled oats
>   (optional)

Blend the sugar, flour, and butter until crumbly, then add nuts. Sprinkle evenly over pie filling in the pie shell and bake as your recipe directs. If the crust topping starts browning before the filling is baked, put a piece of foil over it.

EVA'S MIRACLE MERINGUE TOPPING

"It doesn't fall down or get weepy like meringue usually does if you don't eat it all at a sitting," Eva told me. "With this recipe you can make it today and it will stay perfect till tomorrow."

> 1 tablespoon cornstarch
> 2 tablespoons cold water
> ½ cup boiling water
> 3 egg whites at room temperature
> 6 tablespoons sugar
> 1 teaspoon vanilla

Moisten the cornstarch with the cold water. Stir in the boiling water. Cook and stir until thickened and clear — done in seconds. Cool completely. Beat the egg whites until firm, gradually add the sugar, then beat in the cornstarch mixture and vanilla. Presto! Makes enough for one large pie or 2 smaller ones. Spread it to the edge of the filled pie and put it into the oven at 425°F for 5 or 6 minutes to gild the top.

MERINGUE TOPPING

There's an air of mystery about a pie with a golden-tipped fluffy white topping; you can't tell what's underneath.

2 or 3 egg whites at room temperature
¼ teaspoon cream of tartar
4 to 6 tablespoons sugar
½ teaspoon vanilla or other flavouring
    (almond, rum, brandy)

Beat the egg whites until light and fluffy. Add the cream of tartar and keep beating until egg whites peak. Gradually beat in the sugar and vanilla until the meringue is stiff and glossy. Pile it lightly on a cold pie filling and spread it right to the edges of the pastry to keep the topping from shrinking. Bake in a 425°F oven until it is tinged with gold — about 5 minutes will do it. But keep your eye on it.

WHIPPED CREAM

Because whipped cream enhances so many pies, I'll tell you something about it: remember that cream doubles in volume when whipped; it must have at least 35 percent butterfat content; it must be thoroughly chilled, and so must the bowl and beaters. Beat until it thickens and forms soft firm blobs. If you overbeat, you will have butter — which is fine but not on a pie. Here's how:

1 cup whipping cream
2 to 4 tablespoons sugar
½ teaspoon vanilla, almond, brandy,
    or other flavours

Beat the cream until slightly thickened then gradually add the sugar and liquid flavouring. Beat until thick. For coffee or spice flavouring, add ½ to 1 teaspoon instant coffee or spice; for chocolate, blend a heaping tablespoon of cocoa with the sugar.

Whipped cream spread over a fruit pie, a pumpkin pie, or any other is often preferable to a top crust, but there are always people who say, "No cream for me, please. I'm watching my calories — or my cholesterol." It's safer to put your whipped cream into a pretty little bowl and pass it around to those slim or brave — or reckless — souls who can help themselves to a walloping dollop and spread it themselves over their piece of pie.

Fruit Pies

Fresh or unsweetened frozen raspberries, blueberries, cherries, peaches, apples, apricots, plums, strawberry-rhubarb, Concord grapes, elderberries, gooseberries, red and black currants, raisins. Self-respecting cooks in Waterloo County don't bother with recipes to make regular fruit pies: their experienced guesses provide delicious results.

The amount of fruit depends on the size of the pie plate: about 3 cups of berries for an 8-incher, 4 cups for a 9-inch shell, 5 cups for a 10-inch. Sliced fruits — like apples, peaches and pears — require 1 more cup for each size. Some fruits are sweeter than others and require less sugar; some are more juicy and require more flour to thicken them. For 9-inch pies, ¾ to 1 cup sugar combined with 2 tablespoons to ¼ cup flour or cornstarch and 2 tablespoons of soft butter mixed with fruit should give you a very good pie. Topped with a full, vented pastry crust, lattice strips, or crumbs made by blending ½ cup sugar, ½ cup flour, and ¼ cup butter, your pie will be a winner.

RASPBERRY PIE

My sister Norm has a raspberry patch in her garden, and while they're ripening she's out there picking raspberries every day. She and Ralph eat them just as they come or with ice cream. They make jelly or jam and freeze some in packages with amounts suitable for a pie. Most often she makes a fresh raspberry pie that is eaten at one sitting. She doesn't measure amounts exactly, she just puts things in — sometimes in a 10-inch pie pan, at other times in a smaller one. I'll give you an approximation.

> **Pastry for a 9-inch pie**
> **¾ to 1 cup sugar**
> **3 heaping tablespoons (more or less) cornstarch**
> **3 to 4 cups of raspberries**

Norm blends the sugar and cornstarch, pours the mixture over the raspberries, and stirs it just enough to combine without mushing the berries. She pours the fruit into the prepared pie shell, bakes it at 400°F for 15 minutes, then at 350°F for 30 minutes more.

Norm never serves this with whipped cream because she wants to lose weight, not gain it, but you could do it for a special treat.

PLUM PIE

The pits come out easily from purple prune plums, and a very tasty pie can be prepared in a jiffy. You could use other kinds of plums.

Pastry for a 9-inch pie (top crust optional)
2 cups halved and pitted plums
½ cup brown sugar
½ cup white sugar
3 tablespoons cornstarch (or Clearjel or flour)
1 egg
Cinnamon

Crumb topping:
½ cup brown sugar
¼ cup soft butter or margarine
½ cup flour

Distribute plums evenly in pie shell. Stir the sugars and cornstarch together; blend in the egg and beat. Pour mixture over the plums; sprinkle with cinnamon. Cover with a top crust — vented for steam — or with crumb topping. To make topping, stir sugar, butter, and flour together. Bake at 450°F for 10 minutes, then at 350°F for 30 minutes longer.

CLEARJEL

Clearjel is arrowroot flour, a white powder that my Mennonite friends can buy only at Freiburger's supermarket in Elmira. They prefer it to cornstarch because it thickens faster and smoother and shinier. It comes in bulk. There is also instant Clearjel, which can be used to thicken fruit without cooking.

ADELINE BRUBACHER'S BLUEBERRY PIE

This is a sweetie. Everybody loves blueberry pie; notice how often they order it when it's on a restaurant menu. And it won't be better than this.

> **Pastry for a 9-inch pie with a double crust or lattice**
> **4 cups fresh berries**
> **¾ cup white or brown sugar**
> **¼ cup flour**
> **3 tablespoons butter or margarine**
> **¼ teaspoon cinnamon (optional)**
> **1 tablespoon lemon juice**

Wash and drain the blueberries. Blend the sugar, flour, and butter, then mix lightly with the berries. Turn into the pastry shell and sprinkle with cinnamon and lemon juice. Cover with top crust or lattice. If you use a top crust, seal it round the edge and cut vents for steam to escape. Bake at 450°F for 10 minutes, then at 350°F for 30 minutes longer or until juice begins to bubble through the slits in the crust.

RED CURRANT PIE

About once in a summer Mother made a red currant pie. It had a beautiful colour, like little red jewels, and was tart, sweet, and juicy. To have it is a rare treat.

> **Pastry for a 9-inch pie**
> **1½ cups (or less) white sugar**
> **3 tablespoons cornstarch, Clearjel, or flour**
> **3 tablespoons butter**
> **4 cups red currants**

Blend the sugar, cornstarch, and butter and mix lightly with the berries. Turn into the pastry shell and bake at 450°F for 10 minutes, then at 350°F for about 30 minutes longer.

THE COLOUR PURPLE — ELDERBERRY PIE

Elderberry bushes grow wild along roads and fences and in swampy corners. But the largest — and best — berries grow where manure drains away from a Mennonite barn. The bushes must be covered with netting or the birds will eat the berries before they ripen in early September. When the clusters are gathered and stripped, they make delicious pies.

When the cookie lawyers from Ottawa took me to lunch at the Waterlot Restaurant in New Hamburg, for dessert I ordered elderberry pie. When the owner of the restaurant asked me how I'd enjoyed it, I said it was great. "It should be," he told me. "It was your recipe."

> **Pastry for a 9-inch pie**
> **1 cup brown sugar**
> **3 tablespoons flour**
> **3 tablespoons butter**
> **3 to 4 cups elderberries**

Blend the sugar, flour, and butter into crumbs, and sprinkle one-third of them into the bottom of the pie shell; pour in the berries. Spread the remaining crumbs over top. Bake at 400°F for 10 minutes, then at 350°F for another 30 minutes, or until the crust and top are golden.

Norm and Ralph know where there are some elderberry bushes growing along the roadside; they pick berries every year and put pie-sized packages in their freezer for future reference. Mother used to can elderberries and drain them to make pies during the winter. I always thought them a bit gravelly because of the seeds; I might have been prejudiced because, when I was young, Mother made me help pick the pesky little berries off the stems.

FROZEN PIES

Hannah told me that baked pies get runny when frozen and thawed; better to make a pie, freeze it, then thaw and bake it.

PEAR STREUSEL PIE

Norm and Ralph have a pear tree in their garden that is loaded with pears every year. They give away baskets of them to friends and relations, make pear ginger jam, can pears for winter desserts, and almost every day — while the fruit is fresh — Norm makes this delectable pear streusel pie. They often have dinner parties during the pear season because pear pie is such a treat for their guests. In winter they make it with canned pears.

Pastry for a 9-inch pie
½ cup flour
¾ cup lightly packed brown sugar
¾ cup dessicated coconut
⅓ cup melted butter
Enough fresh pears to fill the pie shell, or canned
pears, drained

Combine the flour, sugar, coconut, and butter. Sprinkle a little in the bottom of the unbaked pie shell. Arrange the peeled and cored pears, cut in half, face down, over the crumbs in the pie shell. Cover with the remaining crumbs. Bake at 425°F for 10 minutes with foil over the pie so the coconut won't burn. Turn the heat to 350°F for 20 minutes till the pears are soft and the topping is golden, taking the foil off to give it a chance to brown slightly. Serve with whipped cream on top if you need to hide a burnt spot, but the pie is good enough without any fancying.

On the day Eva and Hannah and I talked about pies and Hannah gave us a piece of pear streusel pie, she said, "This is Norma's recipe from *More Food That Really Schmecks*."

"It's different," I said. "But it's delicious."

Hannah lowered her head, self-deprecatingly, "It seemed a bit dry so I drizzled some sweet cream over it before I put it in the oven."

GREAT GRANDMOTHER'S GOOSEBERRY TART

You don't see gooseberries very often at the farmers' markets. Eva told me they dug out all their gooseberry bushes because they were so prickly and nobody liked gooseberries much anyway. Hannah still has her's, and she makes a nice jam and pie with them.

Gooseberry tart is very popular in England; I'll give you a South Devon recipe, which, of course, was originally written in ounces. My interpretation works well.

> **Pastry for a 9-inch pie**
> **4 cups gooseberries**
> **½ cup or less sugar**
> **3 tablespoons cornstarch**
> **3 "knobs" butter (use 3 tablespoons)**

Top and tail the gooseberries. Blend the sugar, cornstarch, and butter. Mix lightly with the berries; turn into the pastry shell and bake at 450°F for 10 minutes; then at 350°F for about 30 minutes longer. Crumbs (page 8), sprinkled over this before it is baked, make it wonderful. The English, of course, prefer serving it with custard sauce or with brown sugar and cream poured over it.

GINGER PEAR PIE

With a streusel topping and plenty of ginger, this pie is memorable.

> **Pastry for a 9-inch pie**
> **4 or 5 pears**
> **1 egg**
> **1 cup sour cream**
> **⅓ cup sugar**
> **1 teaspoon ground ginger or 1 tablespoon grated preserved ginger or more**

Crumb topping:
¼ to ½ cup butter
½ cup brown sugar
½ cup flour

Peel and core the pears, then cut them in quarters or slice them. Arrange in pastry shell. Beat the egg, sour cream, sugar, and ginger. Pour mixture over pears. To make crumbs, cream the butter and cut in brown sugar until mixture begins to stick together; add flour and stir until mixture forms pea-size lumps. Sprinkle mixture over pears. Bake pie at 400°F for 10 minutes; then reduce heat to 350°F and bake for 30 minutes longer or until top of pie is golden brown. Cool before serving.

CRANBERRY PIE

This is not a local recipe: it was given to me by a friend who lived on Cape Cod where the cranberries grow. Because it's so pretty, red, and deliciously different, I'm letting you have it.

Pastry for a 9-inch pie
1 cup whole cranberries
½ cup seeded raisins, cut fine
1 cup sugar
1 cup water
1 tablespoon flour
1 tablespoon vanilla
1 tablespoon butter

Boil all the ingredients except the pastry together in a heavy saucepan until very thick, then turn burner on the lowest setting and let the filling stew for about 15 minutes. Cool thoroughly before putting it in the unbaked pie shell. Bake for half an hour at 350°F. Let cool and refrigerate overnight — it seems to need that refrigeration to give it its special flavour.

CHERRY PIE

Norm also has a sour-cherry tree in her backyard, and when the cherries are ripe her husband, Ralph, goes out and picks a bowlful. In no time they make the best cherry pie I've ever tasted.

> **Pastry for a 9-inch pie**
> **½ cup white sugar**
> **½ cup brown sugar**
> **2 tablespoons flour**
> **2 tablespoons butter**
> **3 cups pitted sour cherries**

Norm mixes the sugars, flour, and butter, then the cherries. She pours the mixture into the pie shell. Sometimes she puts on a top crust but usually she crisscrosses narrow strips of pastry across the top; occasionally she sprinkles the top with crumbs made of:

> **½ cup flour**
> **½ cup brown sugar**
> **⅛ cup butter**
> **¼ teaspoon vanilla**

She bakes the pie at 350°F for 40 minutes.

Fruit Custard Pies

*Mother made so many good fruit pies when we were
youngsters that it's hard for me to say which kind was my
favourite. Sometimes I think it was raspberry custard — or
strawberry custard — or any of her fruit custard pies.
They were more delicate and elegant than pies made of
masses of fruit.*

RASPBERRY CUSTARD PIE

Every year raspberries seem to become more scarce and much more expensive. They don't travel far or keep long. You need to have a raspberry patch of your own in your backyard if you want to have fresh raspberry pies in season — unless you are as rich as a politician. Raspberry custard pie needs only a few berries to give it a wonderful raspberry flavour — not strong as a pie made entirely of expensive fruit.

> **Pastry for a 9-inch pie**
> ½ cup sugar
> 1 teaspoon flour
> ½ teaspoon salt
> 2 eggs, beaten (3 eggs if small)
> 2½ cups milk
> ½ to ¾ cup fruit

Combine the sugar, flour, and salt. Add the beaten eggs. Bring the milk almost to boiling point and add gradually to the egg mixture. Pour into the unbaked pie shell and dot the berries evenly over the top. Bake at 350°F for about 45 minutes, or until a silver knife stuck into the middle comes out clean. In exactly this way you can also make

> STRAWBERRY CUSTARD PIE (It's delicious)
> MULBERRY CUSTARD PIE
> BLUEBERRY CUSTARD PIE
> RED OR BLACK CURRENT CUSTARD PIE
> RAISIN CUSTARD PIE (Soak the raisins first)
> DRIED CURRANT CUSTARD PIE
>   (Soak the currants first)
> ELDERBERRY CUSTARD PIE
> GOOSEBERRY CUSTARD PIE
> RHUBARB CUSTARD PIE
> PLUM CUSTARD PIE
> APRICOT CUSTARD PIE
> PEACH CUSTARD PIE

Sometimes in winter Mother made a **PLAIN CUSTARD PIE**, using ½ cup **more milk** and **3 eggs**. She sprinkled the surface with nutmeg and cinnamon. We liked it.

GWETCHA PIE
(Prune Custard Pie)

Bevvy is proud of this recipe from a Mennonite friend in Pennsylvania.

Pastry for a 9-inch pie
⅓ cup sugar
1 rounded tablespoon flour
2 eggs, beaten
½ cup cream
½ cup prune juice
2½ cups chopped cooked prunes
Cinnamon

Combine sugar and flour and sprinkle half the mixture in the bottom of the unbaked pie shell. Combine eggs, cream, prune juice, and the remaining sugar-and-flour mixture; add the chopped prunes and pour into the crust. Sprinkle cinnamon over the top. Bake at 350°F for about 40 minutes — till custard is set.

ELDERBERRY EGGNOG PIE

The best elderberry custard pie I've ever eaten was made by my friend Gerry Noonan, who teaches Canadian literature and creative writing at Wilfrid Laurier University. He lives near Bloomingdale and has elderberry bushes on his property. Every year he freezes berries in sour cream cartons or packages with the right amount in each for a pie.

One Christmas holiday evening when he had invited friends to come for dessert and coffee, he produced an elderberry pie he had made. He told us, apologetically, "It was supposed to be an elderberry sour cream pie from Edna's *More Food That Really Schmecks* but I didn't have any sour cream so I used eggnog I'd bought at the supermarket instead." No need to apologize. Gerry's pie was delicious. And nothing could be simpler to make.

Pastry for a 9-inch pie
2 cups commercial eggnog
3 tablespoons flour or cornstarch
2 cups (or less) elderberries

Blend the flour with the eggnog, gently fold in the berries so they won't break. Pour into the pie shell and bake at 350°F till firm. The berries were floating on top and the custard was sweet, firm, and luscious. Gerry used the eggnog without having put in any rum.

EGGNOG BERRY PIES

I'm sure many other berries could be used just as successfully as elderberries to make almost instant custard pies. Don't be afraid to experiment.

Mennonite Pies

Friday is baking day in Old Mennonite households. It is not unusual to see twenty or more pies lined upon the kitchen counter ready for Sunday when many friends and relations might drop in for noon dinner after divine service. It takes a long time to drive home from church with a horse and buggy. A meal on the way is a pleasant diversion.

Hannah told me, "At home before we were married, we always baked all day Friday."

Eva added, "There were eight of us in the family and two hired men and sometimes twenty pies wouldn't reach and we'd have to make puddings in between."

"And crocks full of applesauce," Hannah added.

SHOO-FLY PIE

Whenever people talk about Mennonite food, they mention shoo-fly pie, which is rather like a cake baked into a pie shell. It is a favourite with busy farmers' wives because it keeps moist in the cellar. My friend Lorna got this recipe for me from her Mennonite neighbour, Mrs. Jesse Shantz, who made the best shoo-fly pie Lorna had ever tasted.

Pastry for a 9-inch pie

Crumbs:
1 cup flour
⅔ cup brown sugar
1 tablespoon lard or shortening
½ teaspoon cinnamon
Pinch allspice and nutmeg

Liquid:
⅔ cup corn syrup
⅓ cup molasses
1 egg, slightly beaten
¾ cup cold water
¼ cup hot water
½ teaspoon baking soda

Mix the crumb ingredients till they are crumbly. Blend the liquid ingredients, adding the baking soda to the water before stirring it with the rest. Mix the liquid and half the crumb mixture together in a few stirs, not really blending. Pour over the top. Bake in a 350°F oven for 45 minutes or longer.

Frozen Shells
If you have space, keep pie or tart shells in your freezer, then all you need do when you want a pie is make up a filling.

SHOO-FLY PIE WITH A WET BOTTOM

I once had this kind of pie for breakfast in Lancaster, Pennsylvania — with an inch of whipped cream on top. A pie to remember.

Pastry for a 9-inch pie

Bottom part:
¾ cup boiling water
½ teaspoon baking soda
1 cup dark molasses

Top part:
1½ cups flour
1 cup brown sugar
¾ cup shortening
¼ teaspoon salt

Pour boiling water over baking soda in a bowl and stir in the molasses. Pour into the pie shell. Mix ingredients for top and sprinkle over the molasses mixture. Bake in a 350°F oven for 30 to 40 minutes. Let cool and slather with whipped cream.

LOTVARRICK PIE
(Apple Butter Pie)

You'll savour every mouthful of this pie's tangy, flavourful, custard.

> **Pastry for a 9-inch pie**
> **¾ cup sugar**
> **1 tablespoon flour**
> **¼ teaspoon baking soda**
> **¼ teaspoon cream of tarter**
> **4 tablespoons butter, melted**
> **2 eggs, beaten**
> **½ cup apple butter**
> **2 cups milk**
> **¼ teaspoon nutmeg**

Mix the sugar, flour, baking soda, and cream of tartar; blend in the melted butter, add the beaten eggs, apple butter, then the milk. Pour into the pie shell and sprinkle with the nutmeg. Bake at 425°F for 10 minutes, then at 350°F till the custard is set.

GRAVEL PIE

Bevvy says this is a good pie to dunk in your coffee at breakfast.

> **Pastry for a 9-inch pie**
> **2 cups flour**
> **1¼ cups brown sugar**
> **½ teaspoon salt**
> **1 teaspoon baking powder**
> **½ teaspoon baking soda**
> **¼ cup butter**
> **¼ cup lard**
> **1 egg, separated**
> **⅔ cup milk — or enough to make a nice batter**

Sift flour, sugar, salt, baking power, and baking soda into a bowl; add butter and lard and mix until crumbly. Take out ½ cup of the crumbs. To the rest add the blended egg yolk, milk, and salt. Beat the egg white till stiff and fold into batter. Pour into unbaked pie shell and sprinkle the reserved ½ cup of crumbs over the top. Bake in a 350°F oven for about 45 minutes.

CANDY PIE

My mother's people were not Mennonite; this was her own adaptation of a shoo-fly pie. Oh boy, and did we love it!

Pastry for a 9-inch pie

Bottom part:
½ teaspoon baking soda
1½ cups maple syrup

Top part:
1 cup flour
1 cup brown sugar
½ cup butter

Dissolve the baking soda in the maple syrup and pour the mixture into the pie shell. Mix the topping ingredients until crumbly. Spread the crumbs over the top and bake in a 350°F oven for about half an hour. But watch it — this bubbling, sticky, luscious thing has a tendency to run over and make a mess of the oven. I made candy pie recently and I found I could eat just a sliver — it was so excessively rich and sweet; my slender young nieces and nephews cleaned it up and wanted more.

GREEN TOMATO PIE

The Mennonites make pies out of anything they happen to have around that needs eating; that's how they managed to invent so many wonderful recipes.

Pastry for a 9-inch double pie crust
3 cups green tomatoes
¾ cup brown sugar
½ cup molasses
¼ cup water
2 tablespoons flour
1 teaspoon cinnamon
¼ teaspoon nutmeg

Remove the stem end of the tomatoes — don't peel them. Slice the tomatoes in thin rings, cover them with boiling water and let them stand for about 10 minutes, then drain them. Arrange the tomato slices in the unbaked pastry shell. Combine the sugar, molasses, water, flour, and spices. Pour the mixture over the tomatoes and cover with the top crust. Bake at 425°F for 15 minutes, then at 350°F for 30 minutes.

COTTAGE CHEESE PIE

"They sometimes pour maple syrup or fruit over this," Bevvy says. "That makes it real tasty."

Pastry for a 9-inch pie
1½ cups cottage cheese
½ cup sugar
¼ teaspoon salt
2 tablespoons flour
1 tablespoon butter
2 eggs, separated
Flavouring — lemon, vanilla, cinnamon, nutmeg
  — or whatever you like
2 cups milk

Combine the cheese, sugar, salt, flour, butter, beaten egg yolks, and flavouring. Mix well. Add the milk slowly to make a smooth mixture. Fold in the beaten egg whites, then pour into the pastry shell, and bake at 350°F for 40 minutes, till set.

FRENCH CREAM PIE

Bevvy doesn't know why this is French — unless some of the Mennonites who came from Alsace brought the recipe with them 200 years ago.

Pastry for a 9-inch pie
¾ cup sugar
2 eggs, separated
1 cup sour cream
½ teaspoon cinnamon
Pinch salt
½ teaspoon baking soda
1 cup currants
Meringue topping (page 9)

Blend the sugar, egg yolks, and sour cream. Add the cinnamon, salt, baking soda, and currants. Pour into the pie shell and bake at 350°F for half an hour — or until it is set. Cover baked pie with meringue and place in 300°F oven for 12 minutes.

Maple Syrup Pies

Ammon Martin had a large maple bush and for many springs sold syrup at the Kitchener and Waterloo markets. His tall, slim, beautiful, friendly daughters used to go with him, until Hannah married Sylvanus and Eva married Melvin. Now they have sugar bushes of their own and go to the Kitchener and Waterloo markets to sell their syrup.

As soon as the sap starts to flow in early spring, Melvin and Sylvanus are busy boiling syrup in the bush. It takes 10 gallons of sap to make 1 gallon of syrup. At the same time Eva and Hannah work hard to sterilize and put all the syrup in cans, which can be put on a shelf and kept without refrigeration.

These are three grades: light is the first run and the most expensive; medium is next, and last comes amber, which is stronger in flavour. Eva and Hannah use it in baking whenever a recipe calls for molasses. Sometimes though, they use apple molasses made from their own apples at a cider mill.

In pioneer days, maple syrup and honey were the housewives' only sweetener. Hannah and Eva like to keep up this tradition.

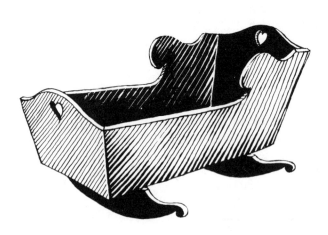

BACKWOODS PIE

Eva says she used the late-run maple syrup for this pie: it has a stronger flavour and is not so sweet.

Pastry for a 9-inch pie
1 cup brown sugar
1½ tablespoons flour
1 cup dark maple syrup
1 cup milk
1 tablespoon butter
3 eggs, separated

Beat everything together except the egg whites; beat them until stiff and fold them in last. Pour into pie shell. Bake at 325°F until set, about 40 to 50 minutes.

NO-NOTHING PIE

"When we were growing up, we always wanted Mom to make No-Nothing Pie. I don't know why we called it that," Hannah and Eva told me. "It's rich and like a custard."

Pastry for a 9-inch pie
1 cup maple syrup
1 cup cream
3 eggs

Beat it all together and pour it into a pie shell. Bake at 350°F till it is solid — about 40 minutes.

WEIGHT WATCHERS

As we sat round Hannah's kitchen table drinking tea, Eva said, "I don't seem to make as many pies as I used to. I think I wouldn't make twenty pies in a whole month. Melvin will eat pie only once a day; he gets on the scales and if he's a bit over he cuts down. The girls sometimes won't eat pie at all. They don't want to get fat. I'm the only one in the family that puts it on. It's no fun baking any more unless you have a hired man who eats everything.

MRS. ELAM WIDEMAN'S COCONUT PIE

Eva says this makes a wonderful winter pie.

> **Pastry for a 9-inch pie**
> **¾ cup sugar**
> **2 tablespoons flour**
> **½ teaspoon baking soda**
> **2 eggs, slightly beaten**
> **1 cup milk**
> **1 cup maple syrup**
> **1 cup dessicated coconut**
> **¾ cup sour cream**
> **1 teaspoon vanilla**

Stir the sugar, flour and baking soda together then add the rest of the ingredients, blending well. Pour into the unbaked pie shell and bake at 325°F until set, about 40 to 50 minutes.

BUTTERMILK PIE

Eva and Hannah use a lot of maple syrup in their baking; they are sorry for people who have to buy it.

> **Pastry for a 9-inch pie**
> **1¾ cups buttermilk**
> **¼ cup brown sugar**
> **¼ cup dark maple syrup (amber)**
> **1 tablespoon flour**
> **½ teaspoon soda**
> **2 eggs, separated**

Stir and beat all together except the egg whites. Beat them separately and fold in gently. Pour into pie shell and bake at 350°F for about 40 minutes.

VANILLA PIE

Wherever there's a gathering of Old Order Mennonites you'll find vanilla pies. "And they're all a little bit different yet," Eva told me. The Mennonite ladies of Waterloo County made dozens of these delicious pies to sell at the New Hamburg Mennonite auction and the Elmira Maple Syrup Festival.

Pastry for a 9-inch pie

Bottom part:
½ cup white sugar
2 tablespoons flour
1 egg, well beaten
1 cup maple syrup
1 cup water
1 teaspoon vanilla

Top part:
½ cup brown sugar
¼ cup shortening
1 cup flour
½ teaspoon baking soda
½ teaspoon baking powder

Blend ingredients for bottom part and cook until thickened. Set aside to cool. Combine ingredients for top part into crumbs. Pour bottom part into pie shell, top with crumbs. Bake at 350°F for 45 minutes or until delectably browned.

Apple Pies

Because apples ripen fairly early in summer and keep well throughout the winter, there are probably more apple pies made in Waterloo County than any other kind. No book with Mennonite cooking would be complete without several recipes for schnitz pie; the variety is infinite because everyone who makes schnitz pie has a slightly different version.

When Food That Really Schmecks *was published, the Toronto Women's Press Club celebrated with a dinner party for its members and me. The entire menu came from the book, and the hit of that memorable evening was the schnitz pie.*

The Italian chef who prepared the dinner had never heard of schnitz pie but he soon incorporated it into his repertiore. On the phone I heard him suggest it as a dessert for a military banquet he was catering. "It's fabulous," he told the person at the other end of the line. "Wait till you taste it. You never had anything so good."

MOTHER'S SCHNITZ PIE

Everyone in Waterloo County who makes schnitz pie has a slightly different version. I think my mother's is the best but I'm darned if I can duplicate her "little handful" of this, that, or the other. I've tried here to reduce it to exact measurements for you, but your guess could be as good (or better) than mine.

> **Pastry for a 9-inch pie**
> **5 to 7 apples — depending on the size needed**
> **to fill the pie plate**
> **3 tablespoons soft butter**
> **1 cup brown sugar**
> **3 tablespoons flour**
> **Dabs of sour cream**
> **Dabs of butter**
> **Cinnamon**

Peel and core the apples; cut them in segments about 1 inch thick on the round, outer side. Arrange the apple slices so they are touching but not overlapping with the rounded sides like scallops along the edge of the pastry in the pie plate. Continue the pattern across the bottom of the pie. Blend the butter and sugar, then the flour and spread the resulting crumbs over the apples, being sure the apples on the outer edge get some of the mixture, too. Dab sour cream over the crumbs, here and there, as well as the butter, and sprinkle the cinnamon lightly over all. Bake for 15 minutes at 400°F, then at 350°F for about half an hour. But look before that — the apples should be tender, the crumbs and crust golden brown.

USE LESS SUGAR

If apples you are using in your pies are especially sweet — Talman, Delicious, MacIntosh — you might use less sugar.

CREAM SCHNITZ PIE

This is richer than Mother's schnitz pie, but not quite so sweet.

> **Pastry for a 9-inch pie**
> **5 to 7 apples — depending on size**
> **1 cup sugar**
> **3 tablespoons flour**
> **⅛ teaspoon salt**
> **1 cup thick cream — sweet or sour**
> **¾ teaspoon cinnamon**

Peel and core the apples, cut them in schnitz, and arrange prettily and closely in the pastry shell. Combine ¾ cup of the sugar, flour, salt, and cream and beat until smooth. Pour the cream mixture over the apples. Mix the remaining ¼ cup sugar with the cinnamon and sprinkle over the top. Bake at 425°F for 10 minutes, turn heat to 350°F and bake half an hour till the apples are soft and the filling is set. Watch it.

CREAM AND CRUMB SCHNITZ PIE

This is a deluxe version. You'll get up in the night to eat that one piece that was left after dinner.

> **Pastry for a 9-inch pie**
> **1 cup brown sugar**
> **⅓ cup flour**
> **3 tablespoons soft butter**
> **4 to 7 apples to fill a 9-inch pie shell**
> **⅔ cup cream, sweet or sour**
> **¾ teaspoon cinnamon**

Blend the sugar, flour, and butter into crumbs and sprinkle half over the pie shell. Core the apples and cut them into one-inch segments, or schnitz. Arrange the segments on top of the crumbs in the shell. Mix half the remaining crumbs with the cream, then pour over the apples. Mix the other half with the cinnamon and sprinkle it over the cream topping. Bake at 420°F for 10 minutes, then reduce heat to 350°F and bake for 30 minutes more, or until the top turns golden.

APPLE CREAM CUSTARD SCHNITZ PIE

Menno Frey's wife served this to her quilting circle and the ladies all wanted the recipe.

Pastry for a 9-inch pie
4 or 5 baking apples
1 tablespoon lemon juice
½ cup sugar
3 eggs
¾ cup heavy cream
¼ cup apple cider
¼ teaspoon nutmeg
2 tablespoons sugar for topping

Core and cut the apples in eighths (schnitz); toss them with the lemon juice and sugar. Arrange the apple schnitz, round side down, in the pie shell, starting with a circle around the outer edge and another circle inside that, filling in the centre. Bake in a 400°F oven for 20 minutes. Beat the eggs slightly, stir in the cream, apple cider, and nutmeg. Pour over the apples, continue baking another 10 minutes. Sprinkle the top with 2 tablespoons sugar and bake 10 minutes longer, or until the top is golden and the centre firm. Cool on a rack before cutting.

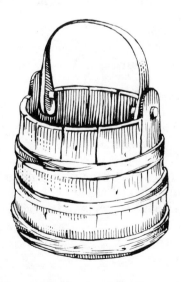

DUTCH APPLE PIE

Easy to make and not rich.

> **Pastry for a 9-inch pie**
> **1 tablespoon flour**
> **1 cup sugar**
> **5 or 6 apples cut in quarters — unless the apples
>   are huge, then cut in eighths**
> **2 tablespoons butter**
> **½ teaspoon nutmeg or cinnamon**

Sprinkle the flour and a ½ cup of sugar, mixed together, on the crust lining the pie plate. Place the apples in a pattern over the sugar and flour. Cover them with the rest of the sugar, dot with butter, and sprinkle with the nutmeg or cinnamon (or both). Bake in a 450°F oven for 10 minutes, then reduce heat to 350°F and bake for 25 minutes, or until the apples are baked and a syrup has formed around them.

GRANDMOTHER'S LEMON APPLE PIE

Aunt Janie says they loved this pie when she was a little girl because it was just a little bit different.

> **Pastry for a 9-inch pie, with a lattice or full
>   covering**
> **1 tablespoon butter**
> **1 cup sugar**
> **2 tablespoons flour**
> **1 egg yolk**
> **2 tablespoons lemon juice**
> **¼ cup hot water**
> **2 or 3 large apples, grated**
> **1 egg white, beaten stiff**

Stir everything except pastry together, folding in the egg white last. Pour into an unbaked pie shell, put on a lattice or full covering. Bake in a 350°F oven until the crust is a pale gold.

DOUBLE-CRUST APPLE PIE

Is anything more popular than regular, old-fashioned apple pie, slightly warm, with a generous slab of nippy Cheddar?

Pastry for a double-crust 9-inch pie
5 or 6 baking apples
⅔ to 1 cup sugar — depending on the tartness of your apples
2 tablespoons flour
¼ teaspoon cinnamon
¼ teaspoon nutmeg
⅛ teaspoon salt
2 tablespoons milk or cream
2 or 3 tablespoons butter

Peel, core, and slice enough apples to make 3 cupfuls. Combine the sugar, flour, and spices and mix them with the apples. Pour the combination into the pie shell, drip the milk, and put dots of butter over the top. Cover with a top crust, fasten the edges firmly, and make a fluted trimming. Cut a pattern of holes in the lid to let the steam escape. Bake in a 375°F oven for 40 to 45 minutes until the crust is a pale, golden colour.

LUSCIOUS APPLE PIE

All the girls in Ruby's bridge club have gone home with this recipe.

> **Baked pastry shell or a crumb crust**
> **6 to 8 medium cooking apples**
> **1 cup sugar**
> **½ water or less**
> **2 tablespoons butter**
> **1 teaspoon almond flavouring**
>
> *Topping:*
> **1 cup flour**
> **½ cup brown sugar**
> **⅓ cup shortening**

Core and slice the apples; add the sugar, water, and butter. Cook until tender, cool, and add the almond flavouring. Mix the flour, sugar, and shortening into crumbles. Spoon the apple sauce into the pie shell, cover with the crumbles, and bake in a 400°F oven for about 15 minutes, until the topping is golden. Keep your eye on it. Serve hot or cold with whipped cream, ice cream, or slices of cheese. No wonder those girls never lose weight.

Rhubarb Pies

There probably isn't a garden in Canada that doesn't have a patch of rhubarb tucked away somewhere in a corner. Norm and Ralph have one; Bevvy and Eva and Hannah have long rows of it in theirs. Since rhubarb grows especially well in Canada's climate, it never fails to burst out of the ground every year with its prolific long red stalks and great poisonous leaves. It is one of the first edible things the farmers' wives sell at the markets in the springtime, and it doesn't last long there, because people are always so eager for that first fresh, succulent taste.

Rhubarb used to be called "pie plant." After going through dozens of cookbooks, I understood why: I found that most rhubarb recipes are only for pies. From at least 60 rhubarb pie recipes, I have chosen only those I like best for this book.

Rhubarb retains its freshness in the freezer more successfully than any other fruit. After it is baked, it tastes exactly as it does when taken from the garden. You can use it throughout the year. Don't thaw it before baking.

NORM'S RHUBARB PIE

This pie has that refreshing rhubarb taste that tells you, "Spring is here! Spring is here!" (Even if it is winter and you use frozen rhubarb.)

> **Pastry for a 9-inch pie**
> **2 cups rhubarb**
> **3 tablespoons flour**
> **1 cup sugar**
> **1 egg, beaten**

Cut the rhubarb in pieces and distribute them evenly in the unbaked pie shell. Mix the flour, sugar, and egg; beat the mixture and pour it over the rhubarb. Bake the pie for 10 minutes at 450°F, then at 350°F for 35 minutes till it is set.

At a restaurant on the highway south of Elmira I had a piece of wonderful rhubarb pie. For years I kept trying to duplicate it. One day I told my friend Helen Henrich about it, and she said, "I know the woman who bakes pies for that restaurant. I'll get the recipe for you." And she did. It was exactly the same as Norm's Rhubarb Pie, but covered with crumbs (page 8).

RHUBARB MERINGUE PIE

This is rhubarb pie deluxe. My guests tell me it is the best
rhubarb pie they've ever tasted: the credit goes to Mrs. Albert
Voelker, an old friend of my mother's who gave me the recipe a
long time ago.

Pastry for a 9-inch pie, fairly deep, single crust
2 or 3 cups cut-up rhubarb
3 or 4 tablespoons butter, melted
1 cup sugar
2 tablespoons flour
3 tablespoons water
2 egg yolks
Cinnamon

Meringue:
2 egg whites
3 tablespoons sugar
¼ teaspoon cream of tartar

Get pink or red rhubarb if you can — it's supposed to taste
better and it certainly looks prettier. Cut the rhubarb stalks into
¾-inch lengths; if the stalks are exceptionally fat you might
want to split them. Measure the rhubarb into the pie plate so
you'll know you have cut up enough to fill it. In a dish, scald the
rhubarb with boiling water and let it stand in the water for 15
minutes (this is supposed to make it less acid or something
equally beneficial — it also takes away some of the lovely pink
colour). Drain the water off the rhubarb.

In a bowl, blend the melted butter with the sugar and flour;
add the water and the beaten egg yolks — the mixture should
be smooth and runny. Spread the rhubarb in the pie shell and
pour the sauce over it. Sprinkle it with cinnamon. Bake the pie
at 425°F for 15 minutes, then at 325°F for about half an hour
longer — or until the rhubarb is soft, the custard set, and the
pastry golden.

To make the meringue, beat the egg whites, add sugar and
cream of tartar while you're beating. Spread mixture over the
pie not too long before you are ready to serve it and either
brown the top under the broiler, watching it every minute, or
put it into the oven for 12 minutes at 325°F. Now share the pie
and bask in the compliments that will come your way.

SOUR CREAM RHUBARB PIE

This should serve six or eight people but three of us kept saying, "Just a little bit more," until there was none.

>   **Pastry for a large pie**
>   **3 or 4 cups cubed rhubarb**
>   **1 cup sliced strawberries**
>   **1½ cups white sugar**
>   **⅓ cup flour**
>   **1 cup sour cream**
>
>   *Topping:*
>   **½ cup flour**
>   **½ cup brown sugar**
>   **¼ cup soft butter**

Arrange the rhubarb and strawberries in the unbaked pie shell. Mix the sugar and flour; blend in the sour cream; pour the mixture evenly over the rhubarb. Blend the topping ingredients until crumbly; sprinkle the crumbs over the rhubarb and bake at 450°F for 15 minutes, then at 350°F for an additional 30 minutes till the fruit is tender, the filling set, and the crumbs golden. This is really special.

RHUBARB RAISIN PIE

You'll like this — everyone does.

> **Pastry for a 9-inch pie**
> **⅔ cup raisins**
> **⅔ cup water**
> **2 teaspoons butter**
> **½ teaspoon nutmeg**
> **1 egg, beaten**
> **¾ cup sugar**
> **⅛ teaspoon salt**
> **2 tablespoons cracker crumbs (or flour)**
> **1½ cup thinly sliced rhubarb**

Cook the raisins in the water until the water has evaporated and the raisins are tender. Add butter and nutmeg. In a bowl beat the egg. Add sugar, salt, and cracker crumbs. Blend with the raisin mixture, then stir in the rhubarb. Put everything in the pastry-lined pie plate and bake at 400°F for 15 minutes, then at 350°F for about 30 minutes more, or until the pie is bubbly and the crust is brown.

STRAWBERRY RHUBARB PIE

I prefer my rhubarb pie pure, but I've noticed that when it's on the restaurant menu, my friends always order Strawberry Rhubarb. We all have our preferences, bless us.

> **Pastry for a 9-inch pie and lattice top**
> **½ to 1 cup sugar**
> **¼ cup cornstarch (or Clearjel)**
> **3 cups rhubarb, cut in ¾ inch pieces**
> **1 to 2 cups fresh or frozen strawberries, thawed**

Blend the sugar and cornstarch; mix with the rhubarb then gently stir in the strawberries. Pour into pie shell and top with lattice strips. Bake at 425°F for 10 minutes, then at 350°F for half an hour longer, until the juice bubbles over the lattice. A dollop of whipped cream doesn't do this any harm.

Peach Pies

Whenever I eat a piece of super, juicy, golden, home-baked peach pie, I always say, "This is my favourite fruit pie," forgetting that I said the same when I ate strawberry, raspberry custard, rhubarb meringue, or elderberry-eggnog pies.

But peaches really are special and are becoming rare. If they keep on paving and building up the Niagara Peninsula, we will soon have only those peaches that come from Australia or the United States.

Don't waste any time. Make a peach pie now.

PEACH PIE

Could anything be more mellifluous than a fresh, juicy peach pie with rich pastry crusts, top and bottom?

Pastry for a double-crust, 9-inch pie
½ cup sugar
3 tablespoons cornstarch
3 cups sliced peaches
3 tablespoons butter

Mix the sugar and cornstarch together; then stir the mixture into the sliced peaches and pour them into the pie shell. Dot with butter, or melt the butter and dribble it on. Cover with the top crust — or a lattice — seal and flute the edge, slit a pattern to let out steam, and bake at 425°F for 15 minutes, then at 350°F for half an hour or longer, until the filling has that glazed, transparent, honey-like look.

BARBIE'S PEACH PIE

Because Barbie has so many friends and relatives who come to her house perched on a hill in the country, she needs to be able to prepare food in a hurry. With a pat-in pastry crust or a frozen one, she can produce a pie in a few minutes.

Pastry for a 9-inch pie
Plenty of peaches — probably 3 to 4 cups, sliced
1 cup sugar
2 tablespoons instant tapioca

Barbie says, "Peel and slice enough peaches to fill a pie shell. Blend the sugar and tapioca and stir the sugar mixture into the peaches. Pour into a pie shell and bake for 30 minutes at 350°F.

INSTANT TAPIOCA

If you go to the trouble of buying a little box of instant tapioca, you might as well use it. It can be used instead of flour or cornstarch to thicken most fruit pies.

MAGGIE'S PEACH PIE

Maggie Moyer, a wiry little spinster who lived on a farm near Bloomingdale and for years sold vegetables at the Kitchener market, once took a ride down the Grand River in a barrel. Often she donated one of her own special peach pies to Bloomingdale church socials, where everyone wanted her recipe.

> **Pastry for a 9-inch pie**
> ¾ cup sugar
> 2 tablespoons butter
> ¼ cup flour
> 14 or 15 peach halves, peeled
> ¼ cup peach juice if peaches are canned or water if peaches are fresh
> 2 tablespoons lemon juice
> 1 cup cream, whipped and sweetened

Make crumbs of the sugar, butter, and flour and spread half of them in the unbaked pie shell. Place peach halves prettily in shell with the cut side down. Cover with the remaining crumbs. Sprinkle the peach juice or water and lemon juice over the crumbs. Bake at 375°F for 40 minutes. Cool. Before serving, heap pie with whipped cream sweetened with sugar and almond extract.

THICK CREAM PEACH PIE

Is it possible to make comparisons while using superlatives — as anyone must who is writing about peach pies?

> **Pastry for a 9-inch pie**
> 14 or 15 peach halves, peeled
> 2 eggs (or ⅓ cup flour)
> 1 cup sugar
> 1 cup thick (or sour) cream

Place the peach halves tightly together in circles in the unbaked crust. Beat the eggs, add the sugar and cream; mix thoroughly. (If you use flour instead of eggs, mix it with the sugar then stir in the cream.) Pour the mixture over the peaches and bake at 425°F for 15 minutes and at 350°F for 35 minutes. Cool and don't let your conscience spoil your enjoyment.

PEACHES-AND-CREAM PIE

I made this luscious pie when Harold Horwood, his wife, Corkie, and children, Andrew and Leah, stayed with me for a few days. The pie disappeared very quickly.

Pastry for a 9-inch pie
¼ cup sugar
4 cups fresh or frozen sliced peaches

Filling:
¾ cup sugar
2 tablespoons flour
¼ teaspoon salt
1 egg
½ teaspoon almond flavouring
1 cup or less sour cream

Topping:
⅛ cup sugar
¼ cup butter
⅓ cup flour

Sprinkle the sugar over the peaches, and let stand. Combine filling ingredients and stir into the peaches. Pour into the pastry crust. Blend topping ingredients. Cover filling. Bake at 400°F for about 10 minutes, then at 350°F for almost another half-hour.

FIVE-STAR PEACH PIE

Radio hostess and cookbook writer Jaine Rodack called me one day from her home in Memphis, Tennessee, to tell me that this recipe in *More Food That Really Schmecks* is her favourite show-off dessert. I, too, think it is one of the best pies ever made. It is not difficult and quite foolproof. You can make it in 2 small pie plates or in a 9" x 13" pan.

Crust:
2 cups flour
⅔ cup fine white sugar
½ teaspoon salt
¾ cup butter or half margarine

Blend the crust ingredients, in the order given, with a pastry blender. Pat into a buttered pan or 2 pie plates. Bake 15 minutes at 350°F, but watch it. While this is happening, make the filling:

2 eggs
½ teaspoon almond or vanilla flavouring
1 cup fine white sugar
¼ cup flour
¾ teaspoon baking powder
¼ teaspoon salt
4 to 5 cups sliced peaches
¾ cup chopped nuts
Whipped cream (optional)

Beat the eggs, add the flavouring, sugar, and flour sifted with the baking powder and salt. Blend, then add the sliced peaches and nuts. Pour this mixture over the half-baked crust and bake 30 to 45 minutes at 350°F. Keep watching it. When it has cooled, slather the top with whipped cream, but you really don't need to. When the peach season comes round again, grasp the opportunity to make this, though I suppose you could try it with canned or frozen peaches.

Pumpkin, Squash, and Carrot Pies

One October morning at the Waterloo Farmers' Market when I was browsing at the Cornerstone book stall, a woman beside me said, "You're the woman that wrote the cookbook, aren't you?"

"Yes."

"Then you can tell me what to do with a pumpkin."

"Several things," I told her. "You can make pies or cake or muffins. In New Zealand and Australia they use it as a vegetable, like squash."

"But what I want to know is how you get it out of the shell to make all those things."

"You can slice and peel it then boil it, but the easiest way is to put it in the oven and bake it till it's soft enough to scoop the pulp out of the shell."

The woman looked defeated. "I couldn't," she said. "Our oven ain't big enough. My brother-in-law brought us a pumpkin in a truck, and it was so big we had to move it to the house in a wheelbarrow."

Mash or purée cooked pumpkin, then make your pie. Put remaining pumpkin into a pint container in your freezer for another pie. Or simply buy tinned pumpkin — more's the pity.

FLUFFY PUMPKIN PIE

This is one of my favourite pies in the world: it is light, golden, and delicate — unlike the solid pumpkin pies that are soggy and so grey with spices that you'd hardly guess they were pumpkin.

> **Pastry for a 9-inch pie**
> **2 cups cooked and puréed pumpkin**
> **½ cup or less milk**
> **3 eggs, separated**
> **1 cup sugar**
> **½ teaspoon cinnamon**
> **⅛ teaspoon cloves**
> **⅛ teaspoon nutmeg**
> **½ teaspoon salt**
> **1 teaspoon vanilla**

Mix the pumpkin and milk, beaten egg yolks, then the sugar mixed with the spices, salt, and vanilla. Fold in the stiffly beaten egg whites, turn the mixture into the unbaked pie shell, and bake about 45 minutes in a 350°F oven.

I have a fairly deep pie plate but I find that the filling sometimes fluffs up and I have more than I need to fill it; if that happens, I quickly pat in a bit more pastry and make another small pie — or I put the overflow into a buttered custard dish to be baked and served as a pudding.

Of course, I prefer seeing whipped cream heaped over the top of pumpkin pie when I serve it — but I find it is safer to put a bowl of whipped cream on the table to let people help themselves. It is unlikely that you'll have any pie left over, but if you do it's better not to have the cream melting on top — especially if you might like to have the pie for breakfast next morning, or — as I often do — two healthy wedges for lunch. After all, pumpkin is a vegetable.

SQUASH PIE

This is another golden memory of my well-fed childhood. Made only in the fall when Mother could buy squash at the market, it has a finer texture and more delicate flavour than pumpkin, which could also be used in this recipe.

Pastry for a 9-inch pie
2 cups cooked squash
1¼ cups sugar
1½ tablespoons flour
2 eggs, beaten slightly
1 teaspoon salt
1 cup milk
Nutmeg and cinnamon

Mother would cut the squash into long slices, peel the segments, cut them into pieces ½ inch thick, and cook them till they were soft. She'd rub the cooked squash through a colander — (till ricers were invented and she got one). It would have been so much easier for her if she'd baked it in the oven till it was soft and then scooped it out and mashed it, but Mother's grand-mother had always boiled it, so Mother boiled it too. *Work* was revered in those days. When the squash was cooked, she added the sugar, flour, eggs, and salt, then gradually the milk. She poured the mixture into the unbaked pie shell, sprinkled the top with cinnamon and a bit of nutmeg, then baked it at 350°F for 40 minutes till it was set. I wish I could have a piece right this minute.

Last week there was an envelope in my mailbox from M. Umetsu & Son, Landscape Gardeners, Burlington, Ontario. In the envelope was a letter from Penny Umetsu.

She wrote: "This past Thanksgiving weekend I entered the Dundern Castle Harvest Home Fair (in Hamilton). My entry was your mother's Squash Pie from your book Food That Really Schmecks. *I am very pleased to say that the pie took first prize. I would like you to have my participation ribbon since it was your mother's recipe. My husband and his father both love everything that comes from your cookbooks. My father-in-law is especially fond of the squash pie. He says that the colour reminds him of a harvest moon.*

"Thank you for your wonderful companionable books. My copies are dog-eared and splattered and I love them. I wish you many more years of writing."

KARRUPS PIE MIT SCHNAPPS
(Whisky Pumpkin Pie)

Can you resist trying this?

> **Pastry for a large, deep pie**
> **2 cups cooked pumpkin**
> **1 cup sugar**
> **3 eggs, separated**
> **½ teaspoon cinnamon**
> **⅓ cup cream**
> **½ cup butter, melted**
> **½ cup whisky**
> **1 tablespoon cornstarch**

To the pumpkin add the sugar, egg yolks, and cinnamon; beat for several minutes. Quickly add the cream, butter, and whisky; mix well. Sprinkle the cornstarch over the stiffly beaten egg whites and fold into the first mixture. Pour into a pastry-lined pan about 2½ inches deep and bake for an hour in a 375°F oven. Try to let it cool before you demolish it.

CARROT PIE

This is another good winter pie. Try it the day after you've cooked carrots for dinner and had some left over. You won't be sorry.

Pastry for a 9-inch pie
2 or 3 carrots, cooked and puréed
½ cup sugar
Pinch salt
½ teaspoon cinnamon
½ teaspoon ginger powder
2 eggs, well beaten
1½ cups milk

Blend all the ingredients except the pastry with the carrots, pour into the pie shell, and bake at 350°F for about 45 minutes. Whipped cream served with this will bring raves.

Raisin and Mince Pies

SOUR CREAM RAISIN PIE

When *Homemaker's Magazine* was 10 years old, they celebrated the anniversary with a competition. Readers were asked
to send in the recipe they liked best of all those published in the
magazine since its beginning. This luscious pie was one of the
top three of the thousands of recipes submitted. *Homemaker's*
had published it in an article about *Food That Really Schmecks*
and me. I have been getting enthusiastic letters and comments
from people ever since.

> **Pastry for a 9-inch pie**
> **1 egg**
> **1 cup sugar**
> **1 cup sour cream**
> **1 cup raisins — light or dark**
> **Pinch salt**
> **½ teaspoon vanilla**

Beat the egg, add the sugar, and beat until the sugar is partially
dissolved; add cream, raisins, salt, and vanilla. Blend and pour
into an unbaked pie shell. Bake at 400°F for 10 minutes; then at
350°F, or slightly less. Test as for custard pie — when a silver
knife blade comes out clean from the centre of the pie it is done.
If you want to make it even more luscious, you can sprinkle
walnuts or pecans over the top or cover the baked, cooled pie
with whipped cream just before serving.

RAISIN WALNUT PIE

You won't get thinner on this one — but you'll certainly enjoy it.

Pastry for a 9-inch pie
1 cup sour cream
1 cup sugar
½ cup raisins, chopped
Pinch salt
¾ cup walnuts, chopped
2 eggs yolks, slightly beaten
1 teaspoon vanilla

Meringue topping:
2 egg whites at room temperature
2 tablespoons sugar

Mix all the ingredients except the pastry together; fill the unbaked pie shell. Bake at 425°F for 10 minutes, then at 325°F until done, about 30 minutes more. Make a meringue of the egg whites and 2 tablespoons sugar; when the pie has partially cooled, spread the meringue and return to the oven until the meringue is golden. Watch it — it won't take long.

To prevent pie crusts from becoming soggy, put the shell in the oven for 5 minutes before putting in the filling.

PLUMPING UP RAISINS

When Norm uses raisins in baking, she always plumps them up by pouring boiling water over them and letting them sit while she prepares whatever they are going into; then she drains them.

FUNERAL PIE

It is traditional for the Old Order Mennonites and the Old Amish to have raisin pie at a funeral — perhaps because its rich crusty goodness lifts the spirits.

> **Pastry for a two-crust, deep, 9-inch pie**
> **2 cups water**
> **1 cup seedless raisins**
> **1½ cups sugar**
> **4 tablespoons flour**
> **¼ teaspoon salt**
> **Juice of 1 lemon**
> **2 tablespoons grated lemon rind**
> **1 egg, well beaten**

Wash raisins and soak them in cold water for ½ hour. Drain. Combine the 2 cups of water, raisins, the blended sugar and flour, salt, lemon juice, and rind, then the beaten egg; mix thoroughly and cook in a double boiler over hot water for 15 minutes, stirring occasionally till thick. Cool. Pour into pie shell; cover with a top crust or with criss-crossed narrow strips of dough. Bake in a 450°F oven for 10 minutes, then at 350°F for 30 minutes.

Raisin pies should be nearly cool when cut — if they have become cold they should be slightly heated before serving.

Don't wait for a funeral to make this.

VARIATIONS

If you prefer, you can pour the cooked raisin mixture into a baked pie shell and spoon whipped cream on each piece as you serve it.

Another innovation is to substitute **1 cup orange juice** for 1 cup water, using **orange rind** instead of lemon.

Or substitute a **cup of honey** for the sugar.

ANNIE'S RAISIN PIE

"This can't be beat; Annie had it at a quilting and it's really good," Hannah and Eva rhapsodized over this recipe.

Pastry for a 9-inch pie
Butter the size of a walnut
1 cup brown sugar
2 tablespoons flour
Dessert spoon vinegar
1½ cups boiling water
1 cup raisins

Over moderate heat, carmelize the butter and sugar; add the rest, mix well, and boil a few minutes till thickened. Cool, pour into pie shell, and bake for 10 minutes at 425°F then at 350°F for about half an hour. Hannah added, "It wouldn't hurt to put whipped cream on top just before you serve it."

CHRISTMAS MINCE

Mother's mince pies are the best I've ever tasted: not too strong and sharp. She made the mixture a few weeks before Christmas; it was always gone soon after and we had to wait a whole year for more.

> **1 pound beef, cooked well and chopped fine**
> **About 1 cup beef suet, chopped fine**
> **1 pound raisins, washed, dried, and cut fine**
> **Currants — but not more than a cupful**
>   **(Mother sometimes omitted them)**
> **About 1 cup citron peel, cut fine**
> **About 1 cup cooked apple cider or a bit of beef**
>   **broth instead of all cider**
> **½ cup brown sugar**
> **1 teaspoon cinnamon**
> **1 teaspoon cloves and nutmeg together**
>   **(careful here)**
> **Salt**
> **½ cup wine or whisky**
> **Apples, chopped**
>
> **Pastry for a double-crust, 9-inch pie**

Mother says, "Taste as you go along."

Put all the ingredients but the wine or whisky and apples into a kettle; bring to a boil and simmer for 15 minutes. Stir in the wine or whisky. Pack in sterilized jars. When you're ready to make the pies, add the chopped apples, 1 cupful to every 2 cups of mince meat, and pour the mixture into a pastry-lined pie plate, cover with a top crust, seal, flute the edges, prick the top crust, and bake at 425°F for 15 minutes, then at 350°F for half an hour. Serve hot.

GREEN TOMATO MINCE MEAT

Mother canned this mixture in the fall and made the pies throughout the winter; we didn't like it as well as Christmas Mince, but it kept longer and was more economical.

6 cups chopped green tomatoes
¾ cup salt
5 to 7 cups white or brown sugar
1 or 2 pounds raisins
1 cup ground suet
1 cup apple juice
1 cup molasses
¾ cup lemon or citron peel
1 tablespoon salt
1 teaspoon cinnamon
1 teaspoon ground cloves
1 teaspoon nutmeg
Apples, chopped

Pastry for a double-crust, 9-inch pie

Put the tomatoes through a grinder or food processor and add ¾ cup salt. Cover with boiling water and let stand for 15 minutes. Drain off all the liquid; then add all the other ingredients but the apple and cook till thick and transparent. Seal in pint jars — no wax needed. When you want to make a pie, open a jar, chop up one cup of apples for every 2 cups of prepared mince meat and mix; taste it and add more sugar if you think it needs it. Pour the mixture into a pastry-lined pie plate, cover it with a pastry lid, making vents for the steam to escape. Seal the edges and bake the pie at 425°F for 15 minutes, then at 375°F for another 35 minutes.

Lemon and Lime Pies

MOTHER'S LEMON MERINGUE PIE

Often in the winter when Norm and Ralph are planning a dinner party, Ralph will suggest that Norm make Mother's lemon pie. Their guests always says it's the best they've tasted.

> **Baked shell for a 9-inch pie**
> **1¼ cups sugar**
> **3 tablespoons cornstarch (Norm's are well rounded)**
> **Grated rind of 1 lemon**
> **1¾ cups water**
> **3 eggs, separated**
> **2 tablespoons butter**
> **Juice of 2 lemons (about ⅓ cup)**
> **Meringue topping (below)**

Combine the sugar, cornstarch, and lemon rind in a saucepan. Stir in the water and blend until smooth over medium heat. Cook, stirring constantly, until smooth, thick, and clear. Gradually stir the hot mixture into the beaten egg yolks, return to heat, and cook and stir for 2 minutes, or just until the mixture begins to bubble. Remove from heat and stir in butter and lemon juice. Cool slightly before pouring into cold baked pie shell.

Prepare meringue with 3 reserved egg whites (page 9). Spoon in pie filling, sealing to the edge of the crust to prevent shrinking and weeping. Bake at 400°F for about 8 minutes — or until lightly gilded — but keep your eye on it.

AUNTIE MARY'S LEMON MOLASSES PIE

Besides the great flavour of this unusual pie, we loved the topping because Auntie Mary always made cookies for us kids out of the part that was left over.

Pastry for a fairly large pie, or 2 small ones

Filling:
½ cup brown sugar
2 tablespoons cornstarch
½ cup molasses
1 egg, slightly beaten
Juice and rind of 1 lemon
1 cup boiling water

Topping (and cookie dough):
½ cup sugar
½ cup sour cream
1¼ cups flour
½ teaspoon baking soda

For the filling blend the sugar, cornstarch, molasses, and egg. Gradually stir in the lemon juice and rind and the boiling water. Cook over low heat or a double boiler until thickened. To make the topping blend all the ingredients into a tender dough and roll it out ¼ inch thick. Pour the filling into the pie shell, cut the topping dough into strips and lay them over the filling in a lattice pattern. (Place any remaining strips on a cookie sheet and bake them along with the pie, but don't forget them.) The pie will take about 40 minutes in a 350°F oven; the cookies about 20 minutes.

KEY LIME PIE

A long time ago, when my husband and I went on a motor trip with Marnie and Charlie Henderson, Charlie said he'd kiss the first waitress who brought him a cup of coffee that hadn't spilled over into the saucer.

It didn't happen until we reached Key West, Florida. The waitress was a dark-haired, dark-eyed beauty. Lucky Charlie. The waitress cooperated with such enthusiasm that Charlie asked her to bring him a second unspilled cup.

We stayed several days in Key West, lying in the sun, swimming in the sea, fishing, shopping, visiting Ernest Hemingway's home — and eating. Every restaurant had key lime pie on its menu. We tried several and I think this is the one we liked best.

Baked 9-inch pastry shell
1 cup sugar
3 tablespoons flour
3 tablespoons cornstarch
¼ teaspoon salt
2 cups water
3 eggs, separated
1 tablespoon butter
¼ cup fresh lime juice
Grated rind of 1 lime
¼ teaspoon cream of tartar
6 tablespoons sugar

In a heavy saucepan or double boiler, stir together 1 cup sugar, flour, cornstarch, and salt; gradually add the water and cook slowly, stirring all the time, until the mixture thickens. Beat the egg yolks and slowly stir in some of the hot mixture to blend with the yolks; pour back into the hot mixture and stir constantly for two minutes longer; stir in the butter, lime juice, and rind, then cool before pouring into the baked pastry shell. Beat the egg whites fairly stiff. Add the cream of tartar and the 6 tablespoons sugar. When the pie is cold, slather the mixture over lime filling in a way that makes it irresistible.

You could make this pie with lemon.

LEMON PUFF PIE

Much less bother than lemon meringue pie and just as good. I made this when Bill and Merna Mitchell stayed with me one weekend, and I made it again the next weekend for Barbie's Easter dinner. They all wanted the recipe.

Pastry for a 9-inch pie
1 cup sugar
3 tablespoons flour
Juice and grated rind of 1 lemon
2 eggs, separated
2 tablespoons melted butter
1 cup milk
Pinch salt

Blend the sugar and flour, then stir in lemon juice and rind, egg yolks, and melted butter. Carefully stir in milk. Beat egg whites with salt until stiff; fold into the lemon mixture. Pour into the pie shell and bake at 400°F for 10 minutes, then at 350°F for 25 to 40 minutes longer. Don't let it go too long. The filling should be puffed and golden but not dry. Cool slightly and serve warm or cool with whipped cream slathered over it if you can take the calories and want to be fancy. Not me.

LEMON PUFF APPLE PIE

This is a great combination.

Pastry for a large pie
4 apples cored and sliced thin
⅓ cup sugar
Filling for Lemon Puff Pie (above)

Spread the sliced apples in the pie shell, sprinkle with sugar, then pour the lemon puff filling evenly over the apples. Bake as for Lemon Puff Pie.

This should serve 8 people generously, but they'll all want second helpings, and then what will you do?

Faraway Recipes

These few recipes didn't originate in Waterloo County but they could easily be made and enjoyed there — or anywhere.

STRAWBERRY TARTE

One day while I was visiting my friend Françoise in Brittany, she invited M. Du Jour for lunch. He is a precise, immaculately dressed gentleman who teaches classics at Concarneau's College. For dessert that day, her cook, Jeanne, made Strawberry Tarte, and it was completely demolished in one sitting. This declicious tarte could be made with other fruit in season — raspberries, apricots, or peaches.

Pastry:
¼ cup butter
1 cup flour
1 tablespoon sugar
2 tablespoons finely chopped almonds
1 egg yolk
2 teaspoons ice-cold water
1 tablespoon lemon juice
1 teaspoon vanilla

Filling:
¾ cup whipping cream
1 tablespoon sugar
1 tablespoon kirsch or lemon juice
1 quart strawberries

Glaze:
3 tablespoons red-currant jelly
1 teaspoon cornstarch
¼ cup water
1 teaspoon lemon juice
1 tablespoon kirsch

To make the pastry, rub the butter into the flour until the mixture looks like breadcrumbs. Add the sugar and almonds. In a small bowl, combine egg yolk, water, lemon juice, and vanilla; pour into butter-flour mixture and mix to a smooth dough. Chill for 30 minutes, then roll out until it is thin. Line a flan ring, a quiche dish, or 10-inch pie plate with the crust, then prick the bottom. Bake on the centre shelf at 300°F for about 30 minutes; don't let it get brown. Cool on a rack. While the crust is cooling, make the filling. Whip the cream, then flavour it with sugar and kirsch. Cover the bottom of the pie shell with the whipped cream and arrange the berries attractively on top.

To make glaze, thicken the currant jelly with the cornstarch blended with water over low heat. Add the lemon juice and kirsch and sprinkle over the strawberries while the mixture is hot.

PEANUT MOLASSES PIE

Lynette Heath, a woman in Guyana who works in the Canadian High Commissioner's office, read my little book *Sauerkraut and Enterprise*, then gratefully sent me this recipe. She wrote: "Yesterday our police band played the Canadian and Guyana national anthems with the instruments that were given to them on Canada Day last year by the Canadian government." She also told me that John Erb, an Anglican priest with Waterloo County pioneer Mennonite forbears, had taken Guyana by storm.

> **Pastry for a 9-inch pie**
> **½ cup molasses**
> **½ tablespoon butter**
> **1 or 2 eggs**
> **½ cup sugar**
> **1 tablespoon flour**
> **¼ teaspoon salt**
> **½ cup milk**
> **½ teaspoon vanilla**
> **¾ cup chopped peanuts**

Line a large enamelled plate or pie dish with pastry. Heat the molasses and butter to boiling point and leave to cool. Whisk the eggs, gradually beat in the combined sugar, flour, and salt. Stir in the milk and vanilla, then the cooled molasses. Add the chopped nuts and pour into the pastry shell. Put it in a hot oven, 425°F, for 10 minutes, then decrease the heat to 350°F and bake until the filling is set and the pastry is crisp and golden, about 20 to 30 minutes. Wouldn't the police band love that? And John Erb, too.

KENTUCKY DERBY PIE

This is always a winner on Derby Day in Louisville, Kentucky, even if the favourite horse loses.

Pastry for a 9-inch pie
1 cup sugar
¼ cup butter
3 eggs, beaten
¾ cup corn syrup
¼ teaspoon salt
1 teaspoon vanilla
2 tablespoons bourbon, or dark rum or rye
½ cup chocolate chips
½ cup pecan pieces
Whipped or ice cream

Cream the sugar with the butter, add the eggs, corn syrup, salt, vanilla, and liquor. Sprinkle the bottom of an unbaked pie crust with the chocolate chips and pecan pieces. Pour the filling over them carefully and bake at 357°F for about 45 minutes. Serve with ice cream or whipped cream slathered on top. A friend in Louisville sent this fabulous recipe to Sheila Hutton.

OLD-FASHIONED SOUTHERN PECAN PIE

Delicious the way Beverley Nye makes it. She comes from New Orleans and is now living in Stratford, Ontario, where she and her husband, Tait Baynard, have the Sage and Sagittarius Gallery.

Pastry for a 9-inch pie
1 cup dark brown sugar
2 tablespoons flour
¾ teaspoon salt
2 tablespoons melted butter
4 eggs, beaten
1 teaspoon vanilla
1 cup light corn syrup
**1 cup pecan nuts — the fresher and fatter the
    better**

Mix all except pastry together with the pecans floating on top. Pour into the pie shell and bake at 350°F for 45 to 50 minutes. Beverley made several of these for our Stylish Entertainment class at Rundle's Restaurant and we all asked for her recipe.

HESTER'S RUM PIE

This is another show-off company pie from the Deep South — the Carolinas, I think.

> **Pastry for a 9-inch pie**
> **1 tablespoon gelatine**
> **¼ cup cold water**
> **2 cups cream**
> **2 eggs, separated**
> **Pinch salt**
> **¼ cup and 6 tablespoons sugar**
> **2 tablespoons rum**
> **1 teaspoon vanilla**
> **1 square semi-sweet chocolate**

Soak gelatine in water for 5 minutes. Scald cream in top of double boiler. Beat egg yolks with a fork, stir in salt and ¼ cup of the sugar. Add scalded cream slowly to yolks, stirring constantly over boiling water. Keep stirring until smooth and slightly thickened — about 5 minutes. Remove from heat, add gelatine and stir well until dissolved. Chill until it begins to thicken. Beat egg whites stiff, gradually add remaining 6 tablespoons sugar, and keep beating until stiff. Fold whites into custard with rum and vanilla. Pour into baked shell, chill until set. Just before serving shave a square of chocolate with a sharp knife and sprinkle shavings over the pie. Pretty good, eh?

Pies Made in Baked Shells

All those lovely pies cooked in a double boiler and poured into a ready-baked shell! Fine for an emergency because the fillings can be made in a jiffy; the shells baked — or bought ready-made — can be kept frozen and warmed in the oven when you are ready to use them.

PLAIN CREAM PIE

1 9-inch pie shell
½ cup sugar
Pinch salt
2 tablespoons cornstarch
2 or 3 egg yolks, beaten
2½ cups milk
Lump of butter
1 teaspoon vanilla
Meringue topping (page 9)

Combine sugar, salt, and cornstarch. Beat egg yolks and milk. Add to sugar mixture in a double boiler or in a heavy saucepan, stirring almost constantly, until thickened. Add the butter and vanilla. Cool, then put into pie shell and cover with meringue.

BANANA CREAM PIE

Make the filling for Plain Cream Pie and arrange **banana slices** in the shell before you pour in the filling; put some slices on top too before you pile on the meringue. But remember — it must be eaten before the bananas turn brown.

COCONUT CREAM PIE

Same basic Cream Pie recipe plus 1¼ cups shredded coconut. When the filling is cool, stir in ¾ cup coconut and sprinkle the rest over the top of the meringue to be toasted golden brown in the oven.

COFFEE CREAM PIE

Add **1 tablespoon instant coffee powder** to the basic Cream Pie recipe or substitute **1 cup strong coffee** for 1 cup of the milk. Omit the vanilla.

RAISIN CREAM PIE

Soak **1 cup raisins** in warm water till they are plump. When you've made the filling for Plain Cream Pie, stir the drained raisins into it, pour it into the shell, and cover it with meringue.

MAPLE SYRUP PIE

1 baked 9-inch pie shell
1½ cups maple syrup
Pinch salt
2 tablespoons cornstarch
3 egg yolks
1 cup milk
Lump of butter
Meringue topping (page 9)

Mix maple syrup, salt, cornstarch, egg yolks, milk, and butter and thicken in a double boiler, stirring constantly. Cool, then place into baked pie shell and cover with meringue. Put under the broiler until the meringue is golden — it doesn't take long.

CHOCOLATE PIE

Sometimes I think this is my favourite of favourites.

1 baked pie shell
3 heaping tablespoons flour
1 large heaping tablespoon cocoa
½ teaspoon salt
1 cup sugar
Cold water
2 cups boiling water (or hot milk)
Butter the size of an egg
1 teaspoon vanilla
Whipped cream or meringue

Blend the flour, cocoa, salt, and sugar in a little cold water. Add this to 2 cups boiling water in a heavy pan or double boiler and cook till it is really thick — it takes about 10 minutes. Remove pan from stove and stir in the butter and vanilla until well blended. Let the filling cool before you put it into the pie shell; serve with a mound of whipped cream or meringue on top of each piece. If you're not going to serve the pie immediately, pour the filling into a bowl and keep it until you're ready for it. There's nothing more pitiful than a pie with a soggy bottom.

This chocolate filling can also be used as a pudding or can be put into tart shells.

BANANA AND CREAM CHEESE PIE

When Françoise and her daughter Florence were visiting me from Brittany, we had lunch one day at the Desert Rose in Elora. We all ordered Banana and Cream Cheese Pie for dessert. It was divine. Because Rosa Lent, the owner, often uses my *Schmecks* books in her baking, I was able to persuade her to give me the recipe. She said she wasn't sure of it: she had just made it up. Several months later, she sent me this in the mail.

Crust:
2½ cups graham wafer crumbs
½ cup ground almonds
⅓ cup melted butter
Dash nutmeg

Filling:
12 ounces cream cheese
½ cup sour cream
¼ cup honey
1 teaspoon vanilla
2 large bananas, mashed
2 tablespoons lime juice

Mix crust ingredients together and pat into a 9-inch pie plate. Bake for 10 minutes at 350°F. Beat together the filling ingredients until well blended. Pour into cooled pie crust and chill. Rose added: "I find that the pie must be cooled overnight and even then sometimes it isn't firm enough — but it makes great pudding!"

BLACK BOTTOM PIE

Wende Gregory comes from Tennessee and this is one of her recipes. She says, "You have never eaten a really good dessert until you have tried Black Bottom Pie."

1 9-inch baked pie shell
1 cup sugar
1 tablespoon cornstarch
2 cups milk, scalded
4 eggs, separated
1 teaspoon vanilla
1 cup semi-sweet chocolate pieces
1 envelope unflavoured gelatine
½ cup cold water
2 to 4 tablespoons rum or bourbon to taste
Whipped cream
Chocolate shavings

Combine ½ cup of the sugar and cornstarch, slowly add milk to beaten egg yolks. Stir in sugar mixture, then cook and stir in top of double boiler over hot but not boiling water till custard coats a spoon; remove from heat, add vanilla to 1 cup of the custard, add the chocolate pieces, and stir till melted. Pour into the bottom of cold, baked pie crust.

Next, soften the gelatine in cold water and add to remaining hot custard; add the rum, stir well and chill until slightly thick. Beat the egg whites, gradually add remaining ½ cup of sugar and continue beating until stiff peaks form. Fold in the custard-gelatine mixture, pile on top of chocolate layer in pie shell. Chill. Just before serving, cover the whole thing with a layer of thick whipped cream and decorate with chocolate shavings.

GLAZED FRESH STRAWBERRY PIE

At seven o'clock in the morning, people start lining up to buy pieces of glazed strawberry pie at the New Hamburg Mennonite Sale on the last Saturday in May every year. Fifteen hundred pie shells are baked in advance, strawberries are flown in from California, women from various congregations sit hulling them in the bleachers of the New Hamburg Arena, while other women put the berries into the shells, pour a glaze over them, and cover them with whipped cream. I don't have their secret formula for the glaze but I think this one is just as good.

> 1 baked pastry shell, or crumb crust
> 1 quart, or more, fresh strawberries
> 3 tablespoons cornstarch or Clearjel
> 1 cup sugar
> ½ cup water
> 1 tablespoon butter
> 1 tablespoon lemon juice
> Sweetened whipped cream

Sort the berries, saving the perfect ones and crushing the others. Combine cornstarch and sugar, stir in the crushed berries and water; cook gently until thick and clear, stirring constantly. Remove from heat, add butter and lemon juice, let cool. When the glaze is cold, put the whole berries in the bottom of the baked pie shell, pour the glaze over them, and chill till set. Serve with sweetened whipped cream over all. This won't keep long — obviously.

RAW FRUIT PIES

Jack Hutchinson, who has a cottage on Sunfish Lake, says he doesn't bake pies when he can simply put fresh raw fruit into a baked pastry shell or a wafer crust.

GRAHAM WAFER PIE

This was Mother's most special company pie, high and so different from the fruit pies we usually had. It was the glamour pie of its day.

20 graham crackers, rolled fine,
   about 2 cupfuls of crumbs
½ cup sugar
1 cup or less melted butter

Blend these together, take a little more than ⅔ of the mixture to line a large pie plate and press it firmly. Bake at 300°F for about 15 minutes, then cool.

Filling:
3 egg yolks
½ cup sugar
2 tablespoons cornstarch
2 cups milk
½ teaspoon vanilla

Meringue topping:
3 egg whites, beaten stiff at room temperature
3 tablespoons sugar

Beat the egg yolks, blend in the sugar mixed with the cornstarch, then the milk and vanilla. Heat over water in a double boiler, stirring until thick. Cool before pouring into the wafer shell. Beat the egg whites with the 3 tablespoons of sugar, spoon over the cold custard in the pie shell; sprinkle the remaining wafer crumbs over the meringue. Bake in a 300°F oven until the meringue is set, about 8 minutes. But watch it — what a shame if it was more than just tinged with gold.

RASPBERRY ANGEL PIE

This glamorous summer dessert was designed for celestial beings: Ruby's lady friends love it.

> **Meringue shell (page 6)**
> **1¼ cups boiling water**
> **1 small package raspberry jelly powder**
> **1 cup, or more, fresh raspberries**
> **1 cup whipping cream**
> **Whole raspberries**

Add boiling water to the jelly powder and stir until the powder is dissolved. Chill until the mixture is the consistency of egg whites. Mash the fresh raspberries slightly. Whip the cream until stiff, reserving some for garnish. Fold the berries and cream into the jelly. Chill until the mixture holds its shape when dropped from a spoon. Pile into the prepared meringue shell, chill several hours. Garnish with sweetened reserved whipped cream and whole raspberries at serving time.

   This could be just as angelic if you made it with strawberries.

SATAN'S CHOICE

This pie really is sinful: I shouldn't even give it to you, but it is a way to use those almond chocolate bars that students keep selling to make money for their hockey uniforms or school trips to Paris. If you make the servings small, you could serve 10. It's very easy to make and better than eating those chocolate bars, anyway.

> **Crumb crust (page 6)**
> **15 marshmallows**
> **4 almond chocolate bars**
> **½ cup milk**
> **1 cup whipping cream**
> **Reserved crumbs from crust**

Melt the marshmallows and chocolate bars with the milk in a double boiler, then cool. When the chocolate mixture is cold, whip the cream, fold it into the chocolate mixture, and pour it into the crumb crust. Sprinkle with the reserved crumbs. Chill for some time until it is set but serve it at room temperature. Your conscience may bother you, but you'll love every mouthful!

HAWAIIAN PIE

Jeannie MacKenzie made this pie for a dinner for eight at my house. We all savoured each mouthful before taking the next bite. Jeannie said she first made it while living in a tree house in Hawaii. You can experiment with the fruit — you might try peaches instead of papayas. Or use strawberries or melon rather than mango.

Crust:
3 cups graham-cracker crumbs
2 tablespoons sugar
½ cup butter, softened

Filling:
4 bananas
Juice of 1 lemon
2 papayas or peaches, sliced thin
2 mangoes, strawberries, or melon, sliced thin

Topping:
8 ounces cream cheese
6 ounces yogurt
¼ cup honey
1 teaspoon vanilla

Mix together crust ingredients until moist enough to press firmly into a deep 9-inch pie dish. Slice the bananas into the lemon juice. Make sure they are all exposed to the juice to keep them from browning. Drain off the lemon juice and reserve it. Put the banana slices flat on the pie crust. Cover with papayas or peaches, then mangoes or strawberries or melon. Blend together cream cheese, yogurt, honey, vanilla, and reserved lemon juice. The mixture can be lumpy or smooth; pour it over the fruit. Refrigerate 30 minutes to 1 hour or longer before serving.

CRÈME DE CACAO MERINGUE PIES

This is fabulous but a lot fuss; try it when you're entertaining the Queen.

> **1 envelope unflavoured gelatine**
> **½ cup water**
> **½ cup semi-sweet chocolate chips**
> **¼ cup sugar**
> **Pinch salt**
> **⅔ cup milk**
> **¼ cup crème de cacao**
> **1 egg white**
> **½ cup whipping cream**

Make and bake meringue tart shells according to meringue tart recipe on page 89. Or place the meringue into a large buttered pie plate, building up the outer edge to hold the filling.

In a saucepan, soften gelatine in water. Place over low heat and stir until gelatine is dissolved. Add chocolate chips, sugar, salt, and milk; cook until chocolate is melted, stirring constantly. Remove from heat. The mixture will be flecked. Beat with a rotary beater until smooth, then add crème de cacao. Chill until it is partially set, stirring frequently. In a bowl, beat egg white until stiff peaks form; fold into chilled chocolate mixture. Whip the cream until soft peaks form; fold into chocolate mixture. Spoon mixture into meringue shells about an hour before serving and chill until firm.

TARTS

Since most tarts are miniature pies, almost any pie filling could be dropped by spoonfuls into tart shells; they're a little more bother to make but easier to eat than a pie if you have a big crowd.

Unfortunately, pat-in pastry doesn't work for tart shells; you have to use the regular kind (page 4). Roll it in 5-inch diameter rounds and fit it carefully into deep muffin cups; Eva says, "A real fiddley business." Which I avoid by buying frozen shells and keeping them in my freezer — sometimes for years.

Sheila, the tart lady at the Waterloo Farmers' market, has dozens of varieties of tarts with fairly thick pastry. Whenever she invents a new kind she gives me a sample, which I always greatly enjoy. She would have given me some of her recipes but it was too difficult to reduce her large batches to a family size. In one batch she might use 4 dozen eggs, a gallon of syrup, and so forth. I think she puts a bit of lemon in her butter tarts to cut the excessive sweetness — and they are superb.

BUTTER TARTS

Butter tarts are a truly Canadian specialty. These are the best of all: rich, gooey, and a bit runny.

> **Rich pastry for 8 to 10 tarts**
> **1 egg**
> **1 cup brown sugar**
> **1 cup raisins**
> **butter the size of an egg, melted**
> **1 tablespoon water**
> **1 teaspoon vanilla**

Beat the egg. Add the sugar and beat again; add the raisins, butter, water, and vanilla. Drop mixture into tart shells to almost half full and bake at 450°F for about 15 minutes.

EVA'S PECAN TARTS

These are a treat for a winter quilting.

> **Pastry-lined muffin tins**
> **4 eggs, slightly beaten**
> **1 cup brown sugar**
> **1 cup corn syrup**
> **1 tablespoon flour**
> **1 tablespoon melted butter**
> **½ teaspoon salt**
> **1 teaspoon vanilla**
> **1 cup pecans**

Mix all ingredients except pastry in the order given. Spoon into pastry-lined muffin tins and bake at 350°F for about 15 minutes. Watch them. "Jerk the pan in the oven and if the filling seems firm the tarts should be done," Eva says.

TAFFY TARTS

Even richer and gooier.

Rich pastry for 12 tarts
1 cup brown sugar
2 eggs, beaten
1½ cups corn syrup
4 tablespoons melted butter

Dissolve the sugar in the beaten eggs, add syrup and melted butter. Bake at 450°F for 15 minutes.

Adding ½ cup of nuts to these tarts before you bake them wouldn't hurt a bit.

BEVVY'S SOUR CREAM TARTS

Everybody likes these.

Rich pastry to fill 8 large or 12 small tart shells
1 egg, well beaten
1 cup sugar
1 cup sour cream
1 cup raisins
Nutmeg

Mix the ingredients in the order given, sprinkling the nutmeg over the top. Spoon into tart shells — two-thirds full — and bake at 400°F for 20 minutes — but watch them.

MAPLE SYRUP TARTS

Pastry for 8 tarts
2 tablespoons flour
1 cup maple syrup
1 egg, beaten
Butter the size of an egg, melted
1 teaspoon vanilla

Make a thin paste of the flour and some of the maple syrup, add the rest of the syrup, the egg, melted butter, and vanilla. Drop into tart shells and bake at 450°F for 15 minutes.

COCONUT TARTS

These are really fancy.

2 dozen baked pastry shells
4 cups milk
1 cup sugar
3 egg yolks
2 tablespoons cornstarch
½ cup grated coconut
Meringue topping (page 9)

Heat milk in double boiler. Mix together the sugar, egg yolks, and cornstarch; slowly pour into the milk. Mix together and cook till thick; stir in the coconut. Cover with meringue, sprinkle with coconut, and bake at 325°F for 10 minutes to delicately gild the top.

HANNAH'S MAPLE WALNUT TARTS

These are like those tarts we used to buy after school from the home bakery. On an allowance of twenty-five cents a week we could afford only one. Eva said, "I hardly ever make these tarts because they're such a fiddle to do." With a gleam in her eye, Hannah said, "But they're worth it."

Pastry-lined tart shells
Raspberry or strawberry jam
½ cup soft butter or margarine
1 cup brown sugar
2 eggs
1 cup walnuts ground to almost a powder
½ cup flour

Icing:
⅛ cup brown sugar
3 tablespoons butter
3 tablespoons milk
1 teaspoon maple flavouring
1½ cups icing sugar

Put 1 teaspoon of raspberry or strawberry jam in the bottom of each tart shell. Cream together butter or margarine, sugar, eggs, walnuts, and flour. Spoon filling on top of jam and bake at 350°F until done — about 15 minutes.

While the tarts are baking, boil brown sugar, butter, and milk together for 2 minutes, add maple flavouring, and blend in icing sugar. Spoon over warm tarts while the icing is slightly runny.

JEAN SALTER'S ENGLISH TARTS

I've eaten these at Jean's and can well recommend them.

>   **Pastry-lined muffin tins**
>   **Boiling water**
>   **½ cup raisins**
>   **¼ cup butter**
>   **½ cup brown sugar**
>   **½ cup corn syrup**
>   **1 egg, slightly beaten**
>   **¼ teaspoon salt**
>   **½ teaspoon vanilla**

Pour boiling water over the raisins; soak them until the edges begin to turn white, then drain. Cream the butter and sugar, add corn syrup and slightly beaten egg, salt, and vanilla. Combine with the raisins. Half fill the pastry-lined muffin tins. Place in a 375°F oven and immediately turn down to 250°F. Bake for about 20 minutes and do *not* allow filling to bubble.

MOM SWALLOW'S LEMON-HONEY TARTS

These were Mom's specialty — and they certainly were special. The filling keeps indefinitely in a jar.

>   **Baked tart shells**
>   **1¼ cups sugar**
>   **Juice of 2 large lemons**
>   **Rind of 1 lemon**
>   **2 beaten eggs**
>   **1 tablespoon butter**

Cook sugar, lemon juice, and rind in double boiler until clear — stirring all the time. Add beaten eggs, stir till thick; take off stove and add butter. Spoon the lemon honey into tart shells or stash it away in the fridge.

HANNAH'S LEMON TARTS

Hannah says she makes these with the lemon juice she buys in a bottle. They're easy to prepare and good, too.

Pastry-lined tart shells
½ cup melted butter
2 cups sugar
1 teaspoon flour
4 eggs
⅓ cup fresh or bottled lemon juice

Mix butter, sugar, and flour; beat in the eggs, one at a time till yellow and creamy; add lemon juice. Fill tart shells ⅔ full and bake at 350°F for 15 minutes, but don't overbake. Just watch them.

COFFEE ALMOND TARTS

I liked these so well at Caroline Haehnel's I asked her for the recipe. I think she made it up.

16 3-inch tart shells
2 eggs, beaten
1½ cups dark brown sugar
2 teaspoons instant coffee powder
2 tablespoons water
¼ teaspoon salt
¼ cup melted butter
1 teaspoon vanilla
1 cup chopped almonds or sunflower seeds

To the eggs, add the sugar, instant coffee, water, and salt, beating well. Add the melted butter, vanilla, and nuts. Spoon into tart shells and bake at 425°F for 12 to 15 minutes, but watch the rim of the pastry. Caroline puts hers in muffin tins.

SHERRY OR RUM TARTS

You won't get these at a church bake-sale. They're pretty special. You might try them with a favourite liqueur, as well.

8 medium tart shells, baked
⅓ cup sugar
⅓ cup flour
Pinch salt
2 eggs, slightly beaten
2 cups whipping cream
½ cup milk
3 tablespoons sherry or 2 tablespoons rum
1 teaspoon sugar
Nutmeg

Blend the ⅛ cup sugar, flour, and salt. Add the eggs and mix thoroughly. Reserve ½ cup cream. Scald rest of cream and milk, then pour it gradually over the egg mixture, stirring constantly. Cook in the top of a double boiler for about 15 minutes, stirring all the time. Cool, then add sherry or rum. Whip reserved cream with the teaspoon of sugar until thick. Fill shells with rum custard, top with cream, and sprinkle with nutmeg.

MERINGUE TART SHELLS

One of Norm's favourite and most impressive desserts is one of her easiest and most versatile.

> **6 egg whites (or 1 cupful), at room temperature**
> **¼ teaspoon salt**
> **1½ teaspoons water**
> **2 teaspoons vinegar or lemon juice**
> **1⅓ cups sugar**
> **¾ teaspoon almond flavouring**

Beat the egg whites with the salt, water, and vinegar until soft peaks form. Add the sugar gradually, beating all the while, and continue beating until the meringue is glossy and very firm. You can't overdo it. On greased foil or brown paper on a baking sheet, with a spoon and knife, shape the meringue into 3- to 4-inch rounds, building up the sides to a depth of 1½ inches. Bake at 275°F for about an hour or preheat your oven to 375°F, turn it off, put the shells in, and let them stay there till the oven cools.

Norm stashes the cooled, baked shells away in tightly covered tin boxes. When she needs them, she fills them with chocolate or lemon butter or with strawberries or peaches alone or over ice cream. There are all sorts of things you can use in meringue shells. All of them are glamorous and delicious.

INDEX